the girl who decided to go for it

the poems of Alice Bromell

Copyright © MMXXI Alice Bromell

All rights reserved. No part of this publication may be reproduced, distributed, or transmitted in any form or by any means, including photocopying, recording, or other electronic or mechanical methods, without the prior written permission of the publisher, except in the case of brief quotations embodied in critical reviews and certain other non-commercial uses permitted by copyright law. For permission requests, write to the publisher, addressed "Attention: Permissions Coordinator," at the address below.
Alice Bromell, Creative Walden
Fairycroft House Audley Road Saffron Walden Essex CB11 3HD
www.creativewalden.co.uk

*To everyone that has been with me on this journey,
be it for minutes or for years, thank you.*

With grateful thanks to

Paul from Creative Walden
for all his help and hard work,
and for believing in my writing.

Chatti Allen for the artwork
on the front cover
and the beautiful illustrations.

Billy Bromell
for his photography.

Fairycroft House

Laura, Alice & Eleanor
at Stagecoach

Uttlesford Youth Initiatives Working Group

Buried

When the soil was above me
And I was in the dark
I used the poetry of other people
To rise from the crumbling earth.
I will never stop reading
I will never stop writing
I will never stop rising
And so,
I hope that the poetry
That lies in these pages
Can help others
Dig themselves out
Of the dark place
That I used to be in.

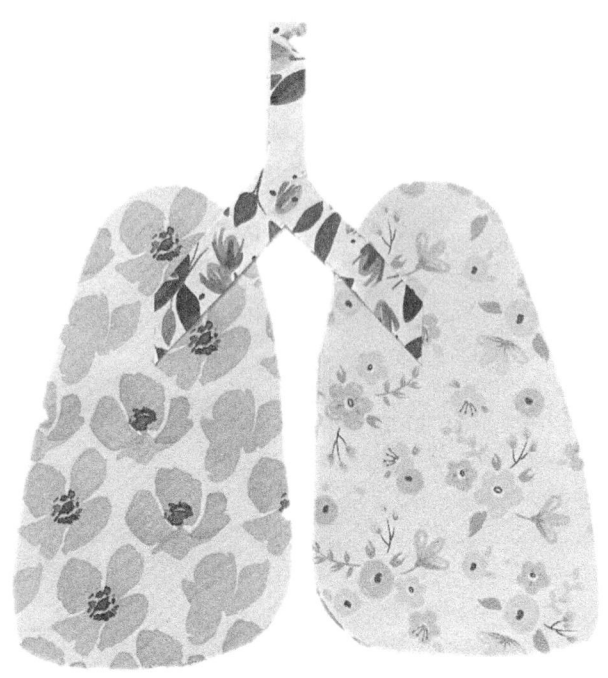

breathe

Burnt Ashes

Just like a pack of cigarettes
You came with the warning signs and the side effects
I took a breath and I could breathe again
I swallowed your fumes and I was whole again
So much more than just a bad habit
I drenched you in fuel
Yet I'm the one on fire
Choking on clouds of smoky regrets
My lungs sink heavier in their cage
And with every intoxicated inhalation
More tangled thoughts twist together
Into the rope of tortuous torment
Dark fog clouds my once perfect vision
It stings my eyes and burns my lips
But the pain, I crave it
And so, I'm falling
Down, down, down to the ground
Like the ashes that used to burn me
I'm an addict
I'm out of control
I won't accept that you're making me sick
Because I'm oh so far from sick of you
So, I breathe you in
Just to breathe you out again
Until I'm reduced to nothing
but the butt of a burnt-out cigarette

I love you so I won't

It hurts me when I eat
And it hurts you when I don't
I'm aching to accept defeat
But I love you, so I won't

This pain that I'm enduring
Is eating me up, pound by pound
How do I tell you there is no curing
A disease that wants me in the ground

Do you know how easy it would be?
To give in to the monster in my head
Yet day after day I face my worst fear
So you don't have to face yours instead

I would rather battle this thing in my brain
So I let myself feel sore
Because although I would love to be free of pain
I love my family more

Speckled Light

Sometimes you are your strongest rays,
That flood the earth in summer.
Sometimes you are speckled light,
That flutters through the crunch of leaves,
On a gentle autumn day.
Sometimes you shelter,
Amongst the vast city of clouds,
And that's okay too.

I look up to you and whisper
That you are the same strong and powerful you,
When you are lost, and the sky feels big
When you can barely muster the strength
To glisten quietly in the distance,
And when the courage you need feels so far away,
That you hide behind the very same clouds,
That often get in your way.
Remember, dear friend
You don't have to glow every day
For even the sun has days off.

Dangerous Driving

Anorexia is in the driving seat,
My wise mind is purely a passenger,
And my body is in the boot.
It's muffled screams of hunger
Go unheard,
Beneath the static of the radio.

A small part of me is worried,
About which road it is we're heading down,
I'm not sure where the breaks are,
And
I don't remember giving anorexia the keys.

The amber lights turn to red ones,
Yet they too are ignored.
Family members hold up 'stop' signs
Signs that are heavy for them to carry
But still,
I can't obey.

Because it is anorexia that is in the driving seat,
An it doesn't seem to care,
About the worn down tread of the tyres,
Or the chips in the window screens.

More warning signs,
This time it's a one-way street
'No reversing' I read out loud,
Anorexia presses down hard.

It feels like we're going a hundred miles an hour,
Everything around us is a blur.
My body is being bashed around in the back.
I have to pretend not to care.

It feels like we've been driving for years,
But we haven't got anywhere.
I'm feeling more and more car sick,
None of this feels fair.

Loved ones start building speed bumps,
And when we hit them we take to the air,
Gliding for a momentary silence,
Before grounding ourselves with a crash.

A sickening sense,
Of heightened exhilaration
Counteracts the fear of the crash.
But the radio broke in the thud,
And my body is still asking for help.

I go with it for a while.
After all, nobody is dead yet.

But,
It's not fun being taken for a ride,
By a 'friend' that sets out to kill you.
It is not anorexia who should be upfront,
But my wise mind and body,
Together.

I envision a crumpled map,
And I find a middle ground.
It's time to stop driving in circles,
It's time for my true self to be found.
It's time to unlock the car doors,
It's time for one of us to leave.
It's time to get rid of anorexia,
And
It's time to take back the keys.

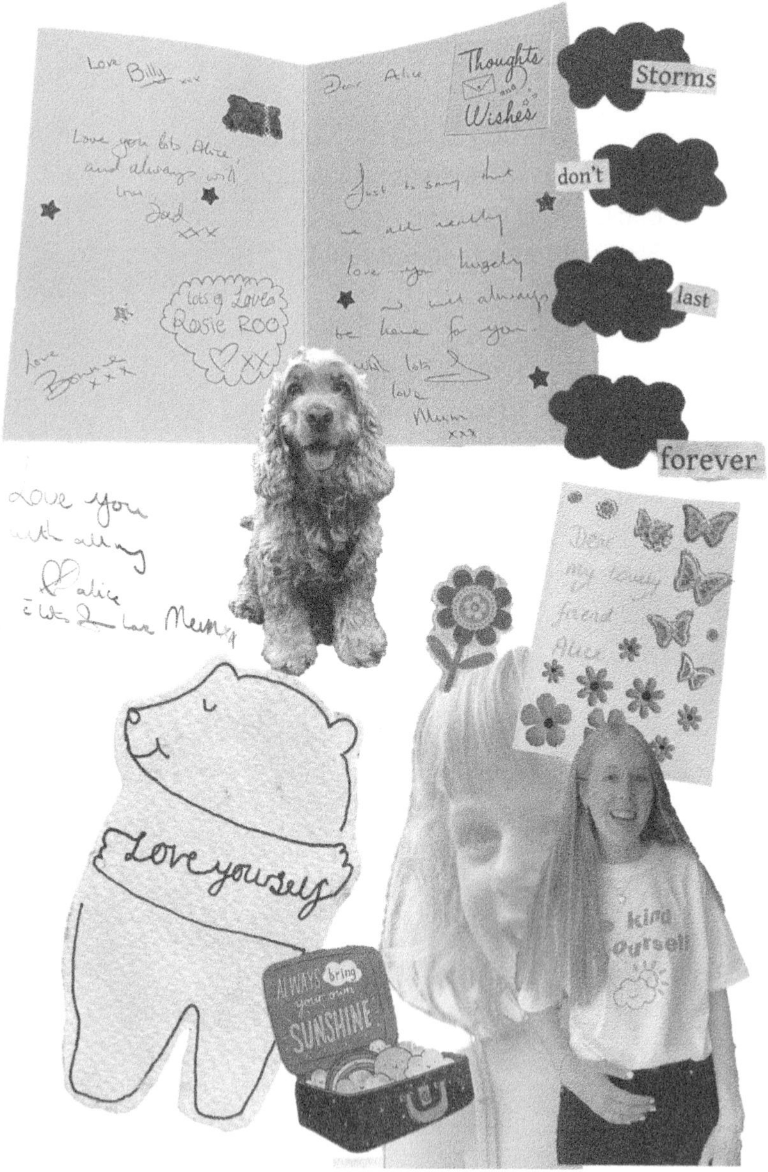

Breakfast

You sit on your crumb-ridden bed
It is breakfast time
You cannot move
You are paralysed.
Too many decisions to make
You don't know what to have
You know what you are meant to have.
You have run out of your special milk
You cannot have the normal one
That rules out the porridge you thought you would have
That rules out granola too.
You settle for toast
You are not sure if marmite is enough
You try to get away with it anyway
You are not feeling brave enough for peanut butter.
Two pieces of marmite toast
You can do that
Oh
You have to have a banana with it
You do not like eating bananas
You have to eat them anyway.
Two pieces of marmite toast
And one ripe banana.
Shaking hands
You open the fridge
You see your special butter
It's not really butter at all
But you can't see your special bread
You cannot have the normal one.
So
No porridge
No granola
No marmite toast.
Banana?
You don't like eating bananas
You'll try again tomorrow.

Reality

My feelings are very real,
Yet I have come to learn,
That my 'real' isn't always reality.
So the next time that I feel,
The ugly sense of inadequacy,
That haunts me day to day,
I will remind myself -
This feeling is very real,
But this reality is not a fact.

Mirror

Mirror mirror on the wall
Why do you make me feel so small?
And I don't mean skinny
Or the opposite of tall
I mean just not good enough at all
You shrink me down
To just an appearance
I know that I would be happier
Without your interference
If I could leave you behind
And be kind to my mind
I would do it straight away
Because I'd rather be a hundred things before pretty anyway.

To the girl

To the girl outside the club
Who held me when I was shaking
To the girl in the college toilets
Who told me I was beautiful
When I felt like I was breaking
To the lady on the street
Who told me I would be alright
To my friends of old and new
Who were there to hold me tight
For all the hand squeezes
For the wise words that I needed
During the times that I pleaded
To just let me go
Thank you, for doing the opposite
For at last, I am beginning to grow.

Piece of cake

They tell me not to worry
They say it will be a piece of cake
But they don't realise
That a piece of cake for them
Is sliced delight
Sprinkled with wide eyes and salivating tongues
Iced with swirls of endorphins
And plated before eager bellies.
A piece of cake for me is
Guilt
Guilt
Guilt
So do not be surprised
When I am not reassured
When you tell me
That it will be a piece of cake.

DON'T LOOK BACK YOU'RE NOT GOING THAT WAY

KEEP THINKING POSITIVE!

YOU ARE ENOUGH

Beating my eating disorder one bite at a time

Just remember life is more than fitting in your jeans, its love and understanding — POSITIVITY

YOU CAN DO IT

YOU ARE NOT YOUR BODY YOUR BODY IS A LITERAL SHELL THAT CARRIES YOUR SOUL AROUND TREAT IT WITH RESPECT OKAY IT ONLY WANTS TO TAKE YOU PLACES

Sleep

As the sun tucks behind her evening quilt
The moon begins to lift his head
To take over watch for the night.
His light glistens on waters calm and rough,
In a moment of simple reflection.
His crescent face softens mine
And I drift into a reluctant sleep.
My mind settles like the midnight sky
And I let my body rest
For I know that the sun will rise again tomorrow,
But that my clouds always linger.

Hardest pill to swallow

It's Friday night again
And my friends are out
Chasing boys they'll never keep,
I'm lying awake in my bed
Simply chasing sleep.
I'm running from the demons,
That stomp to the beat in my head,
The same beat my friends are dancing too,
Except I'm still in my bed.
I'm hot
Sweaty
Shaking, too
Just like I would be in the club,
Yet I haven't taken drugs like they have
And I still haven't been to the pub.
Besides,
I don't feel the high that they do
Happiness doesn't work like that for me
The only drugs I ever take,
Are the ones the doctors prescribe for me
And that's the hardest pill to swallow.

And so I sink

Depression is a sink
Full of dirty washing up
I am also a vessel
Of overflowing struggles
And so,
I sink

An army of abandoned cutlery lingers from within me
Not even the rattle of angry knives and forks
Can escape us from our rigid container

I returned to my drowning
In the rotting, murky water
Unable to answer to the calling of the drain

So I lied defeated
Yearning for a pair of rubber glove wrapped hands
To reach beneath my food stained surface
And drag me from my depths
One distrusting knife at a time

I am warm for now
But it won't be long until I feel
The chill of week old washing-up water again

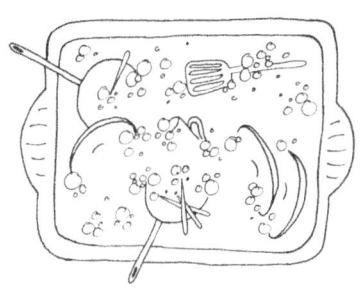

Understand

Go away, stop
You don't understand
Leave me alone, give up
You can't understand
Stop trying, I'm done
You won't understand
Okay, fine
Just hold my hand

Photocopies

We live in a world of photocopies
Unborn lives
Already calculated, formulated, speculated
Uncreated but unavoidably hated
Sometimes the machine runs out of ink
Or the paper in the tray resists
I was born with only half an instruction manual
I stopped printing at age fifteen
So, I took my paper and wiped it clean
Lessons from my previous life smudged underneath
And with this imperfectly blank canvas
I began to create myself

It hurts and it heals

It's not pretty words strung together
by a soft aching of hope
It's not tears that flow elegantly into vases
of freshly picked flowers
Nor is it the delicate longing of fingers intertwining,
Pulling together after too much time apart.

It is instead the clenching of jaws
and the crunching of knuckles
The scraping of plates and food in the bin
It is nausea wrapped headaches
and midnights that don't belong
It is a love so intense
that it hurts more than it heals.

But it is a love I will keep with me forever.

Autumn

Cold air
Skin bare
So glad I'm burning whilst I shiver
The calories from the dinner
That I didn't even eat.

The courageous leaves changing colour
Make the ground look happy and fuller
Something I can't ever be.

Skinny, skinny hunger
Feasts as the number
Drops like the temperature
How long until I freeze?

Tiny bites in coffee shops
Counting steps and counting sips
As warm chai latte greets my lips
The counting never stops.

Autumn's glitter is all around
Yet nature's beauty
Can't be found
When all I crave is thinner

I cannot cease this misery
So, I sit
And wait for gravity
To push its force on top of me
Until I drop
Like an acorn

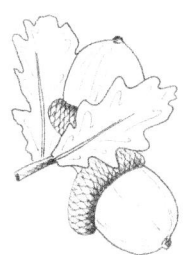

Broken colours

Broken crayons might still colour
But we aren't anyone's first choice
No one reaches for the damaged ones
Their paper falling off
Torn, and curled at the edges
No one wants a crayon that has lost half of itself
And only lasts half as long
No longer what it was
Or will ever be, again

Some of them so fragmented and small
That they are painful to use
Painful to choose
But not painful to lose
So, they stay in the packet
Or at the bottom of the drawer
Where broken crayons belong
Where daylight cannot reach
Whilst the complete ones do all the colouring

Until they snap like we did
Until they break in half
Until they too, are pushed to the bottom of the drawer
Where we are all lost together
In a world of broken colour

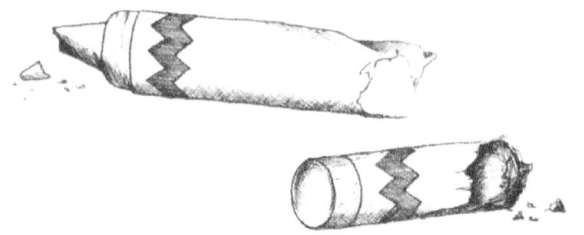

Babysitting

Babysitting might have saved my life.
For it was the children who I looked after,
Picked up from school, gave dinner to,
Bubble baths and bedtime stories,
The whole time,
It was these children,
Who were looking after me.

They hugged me,
Not knowing I needed a hug.
They made me laugh,
Not knowing I needed to laugh.
They made me feel needed,
When all I had felt that day was
Alone.

They taught me that pasta is best
When smothered in pesto,
And that pudding always comes first.
They squeezed my hands,
As they twirled their way to preschool and the park,
Dressed in wetsuits and tutus and fluffy pyjamas,
Just because they could.
I listened as they whispered big feelings into my ear,
about when bedtime should be and shouldn't be.
I watched how they fought and forgave,
How they loved and misbehaved.
And I felt how they loved me,
Despite how I felt about myself.

Every time,
That I enter the homes of these children,
With walls decorated
In chocolate-smeared finger prints,
And scattered crayons
That dance upon the stained kitchen tiles,
(From the slime that we made earlier,
When mum and dad were out.)
All of these times,
That I babysit at these houses,
I come home to myself.

Table-top magic

The warmth of laughter
Rings throughout the kitchen,
As we gather around the pan that reunites us,
After navigating our separate worlds for the day.

When we return home,
We collapse like the leaves do,
After every long and hot summer.
And as the food is seasoned,
we too change like the weather,
As we thaw from the frost of today.

Herbs and spices turn the colour in the pan
From a mundane chestnut to a vibrant orange,
And just like that,
We are alive again.

The aroma dances like table-top magic,
And fills the air with a friendship,
That extends,
Far beyond this kitchen.

So, whilst the dinner is warm,
We tuck in together,
And know that whilst the food is good,
No ingredients complement each other,
As well as you and I do.

YOU CAN DO ANYTHING BUT NOT EVERYTHING

DO WHAT YOU LOVE

the bravest thing you can be is **YOURSELF**

you are capable of AMAZING THINGS

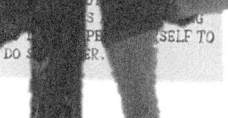

Radiate Positivity

ACTUALLY YOU ARE GOOD ENOUGH
HEALING TAKES TIME
YOU ARE DOING YOUR BEST AND THAT IS ENOUGH
TAKE ONE THING AT A TIME
CLOUDS MOVE
SELF LOVE SHOULD BE GUILT FREE
YOUR MENTAL HEALTH MATTERS
YOU ARE THE ONLY PERSON THAT CAN BE YOU. OWN IT.
ITS OKAY IF ALL YOU DID TODAY IS BREATHE
EACH DAY IS A NEW DAY
YOU ARE DOING SO FLIPPING GOOD
LET YOURSELF GROW
CELEBRATE THE LITTLE WINS
REMEMBER THAT YOU ARE SOMEONES FAVOURITE
YOU CAN DO IT. YOU CAN.

KEEP GROWING

I BELIEVE IN YOU

To my sixty year-old self

In these words that I won't remember
I write to my sixty year-old self
I want her to hold on tight to hope
And not forget the true meaning of wealth

Kindness is a priceless thing
That should be thrown around like confetti
So even when you feel old and sad
You can still slurp on your spaghetti

Be bold and silly for a long long time
And you will come to see
That if you give yourself the chance
Then you too will be free

Don't spend your precious years
On things that will cost you later
Permit yourself to bask in things
That help you to be greater

So, I allow you to grow old
For that is only human
But I forbid you to grow cold
Don't buy into that illusion

You don't have to be the best
That the world has ever seen
But try at least, to be yourself From me, aged eighteen

Beneath the same moon

This might be a poem
But I've lost the words I wanted to use
To describe how proud I am
Of you.
You were the stranger I already knew,
With nothing to gain and everything to lose
You took a chance
On me.
Brought together,
As the path of my illness
Crossed the path of yours
And kept apart,
By the 158 miles between us.
My heart ached for yours
Beating in a ward I couldn't see,
A ward with locked doors,
Fighting the illness for us both.
But
From hurting to healing
From daughter to mother
It is you that inspires me to recover
So I too, can be happy again.
You befriended your body,
And made it your home,
Not just for you but for a child of your own.
As you rebuilt a life for you both.
I look to you, like I do to the stars at night
Learning from you that with darkness comes light
And then I remember
That we exist beneath the same moon.

Tunnel vision

It took me a long time
Of chipping away
At that inky and endless tunnel
Before I hit the rock
That finally gave way
And the light came flooding in.
It filled this hole with a blinding streak of
'Actually things might not be this way forever'
And the streaming light hit me
And took the air right out of my chest.
As my body adjusted to the air
And my mind adjusted to the light
I could finally see again.
And for the first time
Through this hole in the rock
I glimpsed the beginnings of my new life
And I knew that the tunnel
That had been my home for so long
Didn't have to stay my home
Forever.

Bonnie

She is
The golden puddle
That spills into every corner of the room
A charged ball of energy
Propelled by a mighty tail
And wrapped in an amber fluff
She has no judgement and sees no flaws
Perfectly unbothered by the extra-large paws
That she still hasn't quite grown into
She laps up tears
Rests her head on yours
And dreams as your hearts beat
To the sound of her snores.
And as her chest rises
And falls in time with mine
She begins to fix me so that over time
Unlike the toys that she's chewed apart
She patches together the grieving heart
That barely fits in my chest
She is true
She is ours
She is Bonnie.

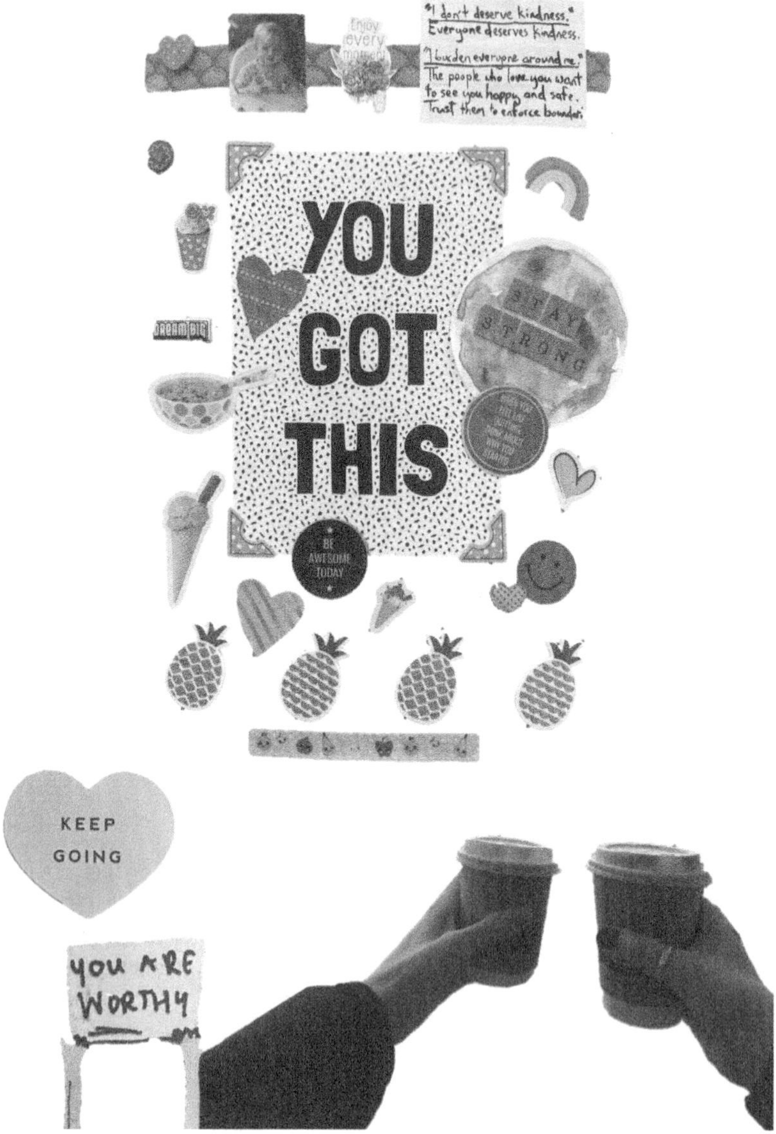
"I don't deserve kindness."
Everyone deserves kindness.
"I burden everyone around me."
The people who love you want to see you happy and safe.
Trust them to enforce bounda
Enjoy every moment
DREAM BIG
YOU GOT THIS
STAY STRONG
BE AWESOME TODAY
KEEP GOING
YOU ARE WORTHY

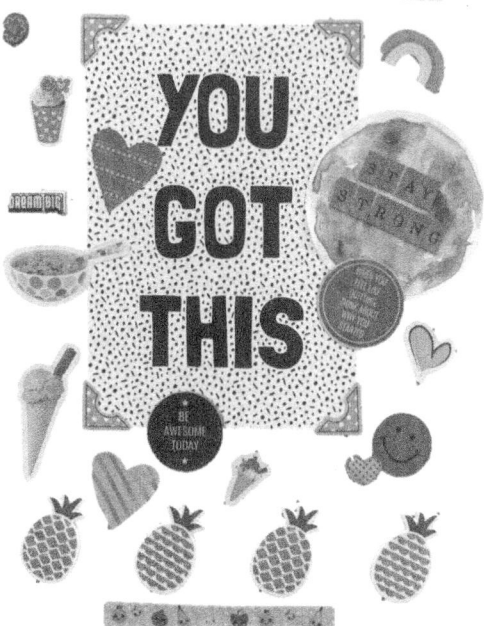

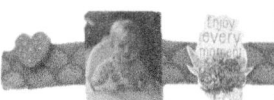

Norway

I promised my sister
I'd write a poem about Norway,
For this is where she dreams to live:
Amongst the noble mountains and icy lakes
And glaciers that give.

She belongs amongst the nature
The tranquility and the trees,
Wrapped up warm with a mug of tea
That's what my sister believes.

So as hope sprouts through the frost,
And birds fly through the breeze,
I want my sister to know,
She can do *anything*,
And be anyone she wants to be.

Daypatient

I've never felt a love so fierce
As I have for the strangers I met online
Where we gathered to bite into our fears
Six times a day
Via the miracle of the internet.

Different bodies
Different paths
United by this roundabout
That some of us have been on for years
And at which others are just arriving.

We smiled when the quiet girl spoke
And clapped when the girl who couldn't cry
Laughed as tears fell from her eyes.
We cheered when someone took a fear
And turned it into a food they could eat
Because they listened to us
And not the voice in their head.
And we sat quietly
When another person lost their fight
As our friend grieved another life
Lost to the same illness that gathered us in the first place.

We bought ourselves bunches of flowers
That we turned up with the following week
Coloured petals in different shaped vases
A promise to ourselves
And a promise to each other
That we will try to give ourselves
What we need to grow.

We built up trust
And unraveled our truths
From the knots that we tried to untangle.
And then together we sewed
Up a patchwork of lessons and light
That I now wrap myself in
When I feel so alone
That I forget I am not the only one
On this otherwise lonely journey.

I never got to say goodbye
Before I got too poorly
And my journey took a different path,
But to all of the girls that carried me through
I hope one day you give yourself
A little bit of what you gave me.

Progress

I used to look to the sun,
In the hopes that it would blind me.
So that whilst the rest of the world saw my flaws,
At least I wouldn't have to.

I used to ask the sun,
To shine its light brighter on others.
So that I could hide undisturbed,
In the shadows of my own darkness.

Now I look to the sun,
Demanding it not to blind me,
But to illuminate the colours of the earth before me.
So that I too,
Can bask in its glory.

I have a friend called Grandad

I have a friend called Grandad
He lived to one-hundred-and-two
He was a little old man, with stories to tell
About people like me and you.

He lived in a place called Custerson Court
In a nice town called Saffron Walden
Before that he battled in India
Where the Japanese had fallen

He liked to read the paper
And talk to the birds outside
Telling them about his medals
Which filled him with endless pride

He was often up to mischief
Hiding toilet rolls when no one was looking
But my favourite thing about Grandad
Is that he always had room for a pudding

And if you've ever made him a coffee
You know just what he'd say
'This tastes like cat's pee and pepper'
And then he'd wink the other way

He liked the royal family
He got his certificate from the Queen
He said all he needed was a good woman
And a shirt, as long as it was clean

He also said 'You must be good
But if you can't do that…
Then bloody well enjoy it!'
And to that, I take off my hat

But his favourite line of all
Was 'Anyone fancy a sherry?'
So raise your glass, to Grandad
And may all your days be merry.

HAPPY READING

The Hedgehog and the Caterpillar

Over coffee and cake
A hedgehog and a caterpillar
Sparked a friendship,
That kept them warm for years to come.

Together they bought magic silver rings
And colourful clothes
And found something good in every day,
Even though some days they had to a little look harder.

They made friends with all sorts of quirky people,
They smiled at strangers with friendly faces,
And wherever they went
People would stop to say hello to the hedgehog and the caterpillar.

And when the hedgehog felt sad,
The caterpillar was there to remind her that she had strong spikes on her back,
And that she was mightier than she realised.
And when the caterpillar felt sad,
The hedgehog told her that soon she would be a butterfly,
That could fly away from anything that wasn't making her happy,
But that everyone is a cocoon at some point.

They learnt that whilst you're never too young to hurt,
You're never too old to heal
And when the world was grey and they couldn't see colour,
They painted their own silver linings
And swapped their old comfort zones
For days that they turned into adventures
And adventures that they turned into stories
That they will never stop writing.

And as they sat and chatted to the birds
Beneath the rainbow sky
The caterpillar promised the hedgehog
That there will always be time for coffee and cake.
And the hedgehog looked to her friend and promised her back
That she was now strong enough and brave enough
To be the girl who decided to go for it
So that's exactly what she did.

BASK FOR A WHILE IN THE GLORY OF YOUR ABSOLUTE BRILLIANCE

BE BRAVE

GO AFTER WHAT YOU WANT OR YOU WILL NEVER HAVE IT.

GOOD VIBES ONLY

I am the flame

Do not say you want to fix me
For I am not broken
I am still the meaning in these words
I'm still the small shine of sun on the frostbitten snow
I am still the hope that breaks into the crisp of dawn,
with every rising day
Do not tell me I'm still broken
I am still the rose that grew from the rain
I am still the heart that beats despite the pain
I am still the bruise that lingers day-to-day
Do not tell me I am the shell of the girl I used to be
Some days I am the dark room
and the four walls that never fade
I am also the candle that floods this room with light
I am the courage that lurks on restless nights
I am the flame that burns despair into ash
and weakness into fight

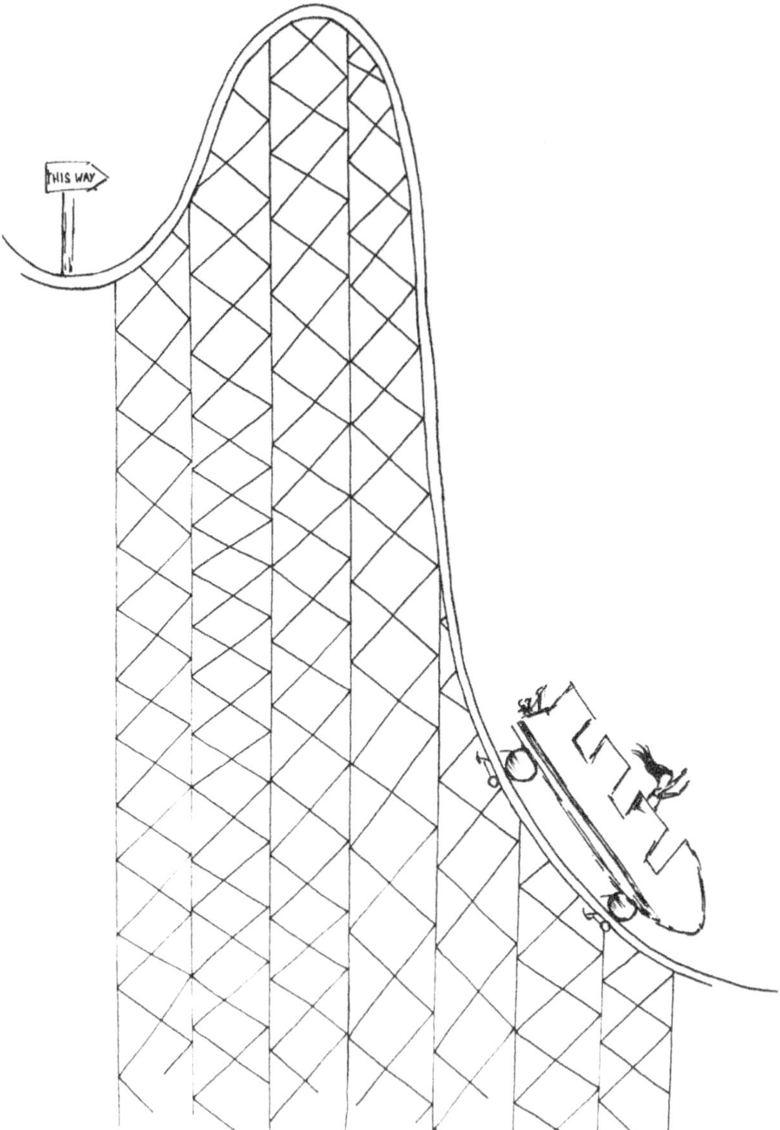
THIS WAY

End of the Ride

'You'll be fine Alice, just be yourself'
I was fine, but I wasn't being myself.
I was 6 years old when my parents noticed I was unhappy at the village primary school, and I was 7 when they made the decision to move me to a school with smaller class sizes and a friendlier learning environment. When I moved, I questioned the world a lot and I had an embedded eagerness to please. From a very young age I was possessed by the poison that I now know as perfectionism. I hated that the class pecking order was based on who had the longest hair or who knew the most lyrics to the latest Katy Perry song. I distinctly remember the time the two 'most popular' girls (bearing in mind we were 8 years old) ordered the other 7 of us from most to least skinny. This was the first time I was put at the top of one of their imaginary lists and I held on to it. I was proud of my naturally thin and athletic body, and I felt as though it had earnt me my place in the group. I was given the compliment of being the skinny one and it felt like I belonged. Unjustly and ridiculously, but nevertheless, I belonged.

Secondary school rolled around and just like a rollercoaster it lifted me high into the air and for once I could see clearly. I took pride in my work and I made a lot of friends. But the 'beware tough kids only' sign had blown off and it was now flapping frantically above me and staring me in the face. The ride took me higher and things became blurred once again; the sturdy comfort of the ground suddenly so far away. And just like with a rollercoaster, you know that at some point you're going to have to come back down, for even the nature of gravity was against me at this point. And that is exactly how I would sum up my secondary school experience — a collision of deadlines and insecurities and fake friends and the inevitable process of puberty all hurtling towards me at a hundred miles an hour. Yet all I could do was remain seated until the man controlling the ride finished his cup of tea and came to unbolt my seatbelt to set me free. In the meantime, all I had to do was not jump off the ride.

By the age of eleven, I had developed a coping mechanism to help me deal with feeling so overwhelmed all the time. I began to pull my hair out. Spoiler alert: it did not help me to cope, and I in fact felt more overwhelmed because I was now battling the beginnings of what would later develop into a form of obsessive-compulsive disorder. By twelve, my self-esteem had dropped and the rollercoaster was back underground in the darkness. At thirteen, I had my first panic attack. My teenage years were the bumpiest part of the ride yet.

Puberty was mortifying. Bumps of self-hatred burst through the skin on my face and purple stripes of anger were splattered across my hips in permanent marker that no body-perfecting product could erase. I knew that the imperfections on my skin weren't going to kill me, but at the time anything would have better than to carry on living with spots and stretch marks. I was devastated; my body, the seemingly only thing I had going for me, had been taken from me, stolen by the thief of life. The anxieties I had known for years were now entangled with mathematical equations and social pressures that I simply

couldn't keep up with. So, I stopped doing my homework, I stopped seeing my friends, and eventually, I stopped eating.
Anorexia Nervosa
Generalised Anxiety Disorder
Trichotillomania
Depression
These were the words that now defined me. They were the labels stamped on my forehead that bled through and left scars that remain to this day. I became a barely walking, barely talking, eating disorder. I was miserable, and yet in the sickest of ways I was proud of my diagnosis. Suddenly the very thing that had consumed me, whilst I was consuming almost nothing, was no longer a secret, and I could live up to this medicalised identity. For a while, I was nothing but my illness.
I flip the TV guide on. 'How to lose a stone in two weeks' and 'Save money: lose weight' flashes up. How can we be living in a world where we rely on tv programmes to tell us how we should be living and what we should be doing with our money and our bodies? I exit the listings and some diet shake advert begins shouting at me through the same speakers that were just two minutes ago warning me about the increasing rates of plastic surgery in teenage girls.
I hear the clanging of cutlery in the other room and my stomach flips as I anticipate my food arriving. ...The waiting part is always the worst.
My mum approaches with my tray, which holds a steaming bowl of pasta — the kind the tv had just been encouraging me to avoid. I immediately compare my bowl to my sister's, which is half the portion of mine. Anger flushes across my face and I begin to cry.
The usual reassurance from everyone watching frustrates me, but that is soon wrestled to the ground by the guilt that has already engulfed me.
I haven't even had any yet.

I look at the food-stained placemat that sits patiently beneath my bowl. I remember making it in therapy and being excited by the future. I hadn't realised at the time that recovery meant sitting with every sickening feeling I encountered and crashing into the obstacles instead of dancing around them. I move my bowl slightly to reveal a photo of young Alice, a huge smile on my face that spread into little dimples in my healthy cheeks. The word 'recovery' in colourful letters above my head was no longer the hopeful reminder I intended, but now so patronising that I glare at it. I want to scream and disappear and run until I could run no more.

My sister has finished and is already helping herself to seconds — a concept so unfamiliar to me that I feel another wave of rage flooding through me.

How is it so easy for them?

Mum's words of encouragement in the background have become words of desperation pleading with me to eat. To just eat.

The choice between letting my mum down, again, and the immediate and terrifying weight gain caused by what looked like 4 kilograms of white pasta was overwhelming.

The eating part is always the worst. I took a bite… and everything went quiet.

As I restored weight and physical health, my family and friends began to see me as myself again. Slowly, but surely, the daughter, sister, friend they once knew was returning. To them, the screams that they could hear above them were now the familiar shrieks of laughter from the thrill of the ride and not the voice of shear panic that I was so accustomed to. They told me that so long as I stayed on track I would get there, I just had to trust them.

But how could I trust them when I couldn't even see the track I was supposed to be following? As much as I wanted to be better, and not have these thoughts engraved into my brain, it was hard trying to recover in a world that promotes diet culture and profits off insecurities.

I was being told to eat up and gain weight, whilst everyone else was 'being good' and 'watching their weight'. I wasn't allowed to exercise, yet I had to watch whilst everyone else paced around the living room trying to get in their 10,000 steps a day, that some watch on their wrist had guilt-tripped them into doing. It was like trying to erase an inky dribble of pen but before I had even unwritten the first few letters, diet culture came along and re-scribbled the words all over again, in an even harsher pen. In the end, all I was left with was a state of confusion in the form of an inky and illegible smudge. No one understood.

We had people round for tea and whilst I sat there picking at the huge slab of cake I'd been given, 'because that's what's on my meal plan', our visitors turned down the cake and settled for a black coffee, because now even milk was too fattening. They said it was about physical health and looking after their bodies, But what about mental health and enjoyment?

Summer was approaching and the only reason they were depriving themselves, via yet another diet, was all for something as shallow as having what they called a 'beach body'. The kind of body I wasn't allowed to have. I wanted to scream. There was so much I wish people knew. I wished people would abolish this idyllic perfect body and realise that the pouch of fat on our stomachs exist to protect our organs, it doesn't make you a better person because your thighs don't touch, and there are worse things in life than having bingo wings.

These kinds of comments did stop for a while when I was visibly underweight, yet the moment I seemed 'ok' again, their feet parted from the brakes and the comments came crashing in, with no idea that these were the kinds of words that built up and up and up into the ride I was STILL trying to recover from. Still, the filters were removed, and no comment was left uncensored. Not even the ones about ME, or the way I looked.

I desperately wanted the comments on my body to stop and my size to NOT be judged in a way that dictated the severity of my illness. I wanted the comparisons to end, and I didn't want to

hear about someone else who was suffering, but 'much worse' than I was. I wanted people to know that even with an identical diagnosis, no track is ever the same, but that any brain with an eating disorder is an unhealthy one and anyone who suffers is already sick enough. I wanted to shout that waiting until someone is 'visibly unhealthy' is the most harmful thing we can do. They didn't get that just because you look fine, doesn't mean you are. How did they not understand that there could be upset and terror concealed within the louder shrieks of joy heard as the rollercoaster flies down the tracks, yet no one knows which ones are which. I tried to explain that someone who is sick with exhaustion might shrug it off as temporary motion sickness, before compulsively buying another ticket and climbing the ride all over again. I described the never-ending haze of numbness that some people experience, I knew not everyone would be able to relate to the highs and lows of the ride that I felt so deeply. I used up so much of my energy trying to educate others, it only left me more devastated. I knew then that I had no option but to block out the noise of those on completely different rides, and for once I just had to focus on my own. I had to accept that not everyone would understand, but I had to put myself first regardless. After all, this was the ride I was stuck on, and I wanted to make the rest of my time on it a nice place to be. My mind was still clouded by the smoke from beneath my wheels, it shadowed my every move and chased my breathing corpse. Every sharp turn caught me off guard and just as I thought I was finally getting somewhere, my world would be thrown upside down again.

There was no way I could continue living like this, it was time to find a new ride. I did one last loop de loop, convincing myself this wasn't what I wanted. And that's when I slammed on the breaks.

The law of physics dictates that, in regards to emergency breaks, trying to put a sudden stop to all motion, whilst still in the process of slicing through the air at full speed, the odds will never be in your favour.

It is not as simple as coming slowly to a halt and peacefully stepping off. I envisioned myself flying off the edge when the track took its next turn and shuddered as I planned to leave the familiar behind. Nevertheless, I willed the cart to propel me as I plunged into the most terrifying thing ever...the unknown.

Thank god there were people there to catch me. Everybody kept banging on about this recovery thing and how life would be so much better again if I just started trying, as if I wasn't trying already. They said they wanted the old me back, unaware that the happy face they remember was one that I painted on every day for years, and a face I hid when the paint started to drip. I didn't want recovery to be about going back to the ride I was on before I got sick; just because it appeared flatter and more stable doesn't mean it felt safe to me. I wanted permission to build a new ride, to finally become the person I needed when I was younger.

I knew I had all the skills lurking somewhere within me and with the right tools, maybe I was capable of creating a path to suit me and what I want my life to be, one that would stop me from getting sick again. I knew it might not be as smooth a ride as my old one but this one would have the advantage of more secure boundaries, stronger suspension, and the addition of good people beside me.

Even comfier seats make a difference when you're trying to find peace within your home, within your body. I didn't want to remain a passenger on my own ride, I wanted to drive it and be in control of the inevitable highs and lows. Loved ones were still holding up stop signs that were heavy for them to carry and building speed bumps in attempt to slow down the progression of my illness, but it was only I who could take the wheel and slam my wobbly feet down on the brakes. I felt angry for them, that I couldn't just get on with it.

After all, I might be the one that bought the ticket, but they're all stuck at this theme park with me, fatigued by the unpredictability of the rides. I had to get myself out of here, so I could also set them free.

I despised sitting in the waiting room at the clinic I attended sometimes several times a week. It wasn't just me that was a barely walking, barely talking eating disorder in there. We all were. The minute I walked in, I immediately noted the sizes of my competitors and then cast my eyes to my own shrunken thighs. I wanted to hug them all and tell them they would be okay, but at the same time I felt a sickening thread of jealousy shoot through me every time I laid eyes on someone smaller than me.

None of us spoke, in fact we barely smiled, each one of us falling victim to the same silent game of comparison. I never stopped dreading the minutes sat in that bleak waiting room, each time unsure what version of an eating disorder I would come face to face with. Over time, I met more versions of eating disorders than I knew existed. It wasn't just skinny white teenage girls, in fact, sometimes I was the only cliché in there. I walked through the same doors and sat in the same seats that those in older, younger, physically healthy bodies did, and saw weight loss for just the side effect it is, not the actual monster itself. I shared sad glances and knowing looks with people of every colour, class and creed. We didn't all share the same stereotypical appearance, but we all carried the same hurt, the same pain. And that made us more connected than any identical surface ever could.

When I was sixteen, my team at the children and adolescent mental health services helped me to formulate a plan. From my very first days in therapy we would draw Venn diagrams so that we could visualise the proportion of good stuff to bad stuff, the real me to the ill parts of me, Alice to anorexia. One session, my (incredible) eating disorder nurse explained to me that although my anorexia was getting weaker and I was getting stronger, it would be difficult to keep strengthening the Alice part of me, whilst my entire identity was based around being so poorly. Therefore, in order to shrink the bad stuff, we had to grow all the goodness that was apparently hiding somewhere within me. A bit like when the rollercoaster jolts unpredictably, and you fly forwards in your seat; your breath stuck in your chest — her next question caught me off guard.

'Who is Alice? I have come to learn the complexities of your disorder, I understand every tip and trick that it has up its sleeve, and I believe you know it just as well yourself.'

She was right, I did.

'But, there is a girl underneath all of that, who is she?'

I had no idea that I could be something greater than the pain that I had morphed into. I had never known anything different. I wasn't sure I was ready for anything different. On the car journey home, I remember sipping on my Fortisip: a disgusting, calorific, nutrient-dense supplement drink that soon became known in our family as the dreaded 'Fortishit', and I remember promising myself I would make a conscious effort to free myself of this never-ending cycle of appointments and therapy and check-ups and blood tests and weigh ins. I spent every waking moment of my day with knuckles whiter than winter frost; already anticipating the next dip before it happens. I imagined the girl I could be, if only I gave myself a chance. What a radical thing to imagine.

So, I stopped feeding my eating disorder and I started feeding myself. I starved myself not of food but of self-hatred. I started spending less time counting calories and more time counting the chocolate chips in my ice cream. I stopped comparing the macronutrients in different food types and started learning which foods I actually liked the taste of. And then I ate those foods. I left the house for more than just appointments, I joined in when my siblings had cakes after school on a Friday, and I ran about with my dog in the sunshine not to burn calories but to feel the warmth of happiness upon my now glowing skin. I spent less time in my room pulling my hair out and more time filling the pages of my recovery scrapbook, cutting out notes from my friends and reminders from my doctors, and sticking them in with an array of patterned tape and funky stickers. I made a mess on Mum's carpet, but it didn't matter because I now had the energy to clear it up. The chunks of hair that used to jam the hoover were now snippets of colour that hadn't quite made it onto the paper. I wrote poetry not just about the darkness I had known so well but also the light that I was making friends with. I stopped leaving food on my plate and started leaving my comfort zone instead. I volunteered at the preschool in my village and spent my mornings laughing with three-year olds. I befriended a 101-year old man and listened whilst he told the same stories over and over again. I outgrew my clothes and instead of demanding my body to shrink into them like I silently craved it would, I bought new clothes that would fit my new body. Eventually, I threw the old clothes out. I was no longer neglecting my own needs but instead doing everything in my power to nourish the person I had trampled on for so long. I wish I could say I did all of this with my hands in the air and my head held high, but the truth is I spent most of the ride crying into someone's lap. Now I feel all the more courageous for it.

I always knew the calm moments of stillness and peace were short-lived, but I now know that the slow climb to the grind of chains and the rapid declines are also temporary, and more times that than not the ride is shorter than you had ever realised. I have come to learn that life can take your breath away, but in the most beautiful of ways as well as the cruellest. Perhaps I didn't quite reach the height restrictions for the emotional rollercoaster that was my teenage years, but there is no age limit on grief like that. No one can ever prepare to mourn the loss of their own identity. I am worth more than a friendship based solely on my appearance, I am capable of more than contorting my body into a shape created by the photoshop-armed media, and the number on the scales will never be high enough to account for all of what I am.

So, I ask myself again – who am I?

I am Alice, I'm eighteen years old and I am building the most beautiful life for myself. I love charity shops and rainbows and choc-chip ice cream in summer, and winter. I am healthy and I am so very nearly happy. I am alive and burning with ambition. I hope I am someone my eight-year old self would be fiercely proud of. I have a passion for poetry, a desire for creativity and a hunger for life that will never be silenced by appetite suppressants.

I am the girl who decided to go for it. I am Alice.

It's not easy for me to say that this wasn't the end of my ride. Healing is never linear and recovery from an eating disorder is not a one-time decision - you have to choose it over and over and over again, both when you feel ready for it and when you don't. And most of the time you don't.

Just as you live with an eating disorder, you live with recovery; you're not at the theme park for the day. Your first set of tracks is behind you, but it's not too late to carve the track ahead into something that you finally enjoy following. So, take a seat and climb up high, and when you reach the clouds paint your name in gold beneath their already silver linings, and be the one that decides to go for it.

ALICE (CONT'D)

I am Alice,
I'm eighteen years old
and I am building the most beautiful life for myself.
I love charity shops and rainbows
and choc-chip ice cream in summer,
and hot soup in winter.
I am healthier and I am happier than ever before.
I am alive and burning with ambition.
I hope I am someone
my eight-year-old self would be fiercely proud of.
I have a passion for poetry, a desire for creativity
and a hunger for life
that will never be silenced by appetite suppressants.

ALICE stops abruptly and pauses.

ALICE (CONT'D)

I am the girl who decided to go for it.
I am Alice.

EXT. FUNFAIR – DAY

ALICE is on a rollercoaster, surrounded
the air and screaming with joy.
of the funfair fades.

ALICE THE WRIT
It's not easy for me to say
this wasn't the end of my r
Healing is never linear
and recovery from an eat
is not a one-time decis
– you have to choose
both when you feel r
and when you don't.
Just as you live w
you're not at t
your first set
but it's not
something t
So, take a
and when
beneath
and be

Eleanor Armstrong performs Teenage Alice in the audio play 'ALICE' based on 'End of the Ride'.

ALICE

V3J
AUGUST 2021

AUDIO PLAY

Written by

Alice Bromell

Director / Producer: Paul Bellany
(Creative Walden)

Director: Laura Sommerville
(Stagecoach Principal)

Creative Walden
Fairycroft House
43 Audley Road
Saffron Walden
Essex
CB11 3BD

Info@creativewalden.co.uk

Alice Mandl plays the voice of Young Alice

PLAYGROUND – DAY

s and girls running around and playing games in
ool Playground. In the foreground some kids are
kipping game.

YOUNG KIDS
in the gang? Who's a left out?
gonna cry and scream and shout?

1, 2, 3, 4,
Here comes Sam, like a millionaire,
He's so pretty and she's got long hair,
Go, Sam, jump, Sam; Jump, jump, jump,
She's so pretty, tall and slim,
Here comes Alice; Jump, jump, jump,
Put her at the front 'cca she's so thin,
Jump, Alice, jump, Alice; jump, jump, JUMP

The last "Jump" is emphasised.

OL PLAYGROUND – DAY
CE, stands in wide-eyed trepidation
fence, kids play and runaround
arts off blurred then sharp